W9-AWJ-326

I LIVE IN ISRAEL

I LIVE IN ISRAEL

A Text and Activity Book

MAX FRANKEL AND JUDY HOFFMAN

BEHRMAN HOUSE, INC., PUBLISHERS, NEW YORK, N.Y.

Designer: Hananya Cohen   Illustrator: Naama Nothman
Project Editor: Priscilla Fishman

Copyright © 1979, by Max Frankel and Judy Hoffman
Published by Behrman House, Inc., 1261 Broadway, New York, N.Y. 10001

Library of Congress Cataloging in Publication Data

Frankel, Max, 1914-
  I live in Israel.

  1. Israel—Juvenile literature. I. Hoffman,
Judy, joint author. II. Title.
DS126.5.F72 956.94 79-12833
ISBN 0-87441-317-6

MANUFACTURED IN THE UNITED STATES OF AMERICA

We, who grew up with the dream of a State of Israel,

dedicate this book to today's children,

who are witnessing the fulfillment of that dream —

and to the unborn generations of children

who will be privileged to come into a world

where Israel will continue to play an important role

in their growth and development.

PICTURE CREDITS

AZYF, 119.   Max Frankel, 73.

Israel Government Press Office, 16, 18, 27, 32, 39, 40, 52, 53, 55, 56, 57, 63, 64, 71, 72, 74, 75, 82, 83, 84, 120, 121, 122.

Israel Museum, 43, 44; 45.

Israel Tourist Office, 17, 25, 30, 31, 38, 54, 62, 65, 66, 81, 82, 91, 92, 93, 94, 95, 101.

Jewish National Fund, 16, 44, 94, 112, 120, 121.

Keren Hayesod, 15, 25, 26, 28, 41, 42, 54, 57, 74, 90, 103, 122.

Dr. Kurt Meyerowitz, 33, 38.   Zev Radovan, frontispiece.

The prints on pages 110 and 113 are from **Israel: Twenty Graphic Prints by Jewish and Arab Children** (Rubin Mass, Jerusalem). We acknowledge with thanks the kindness of Dr. Puah Menczel (editor) and of the Dr. J.S. Menczel Memorial Foundation, in granting permission to reproduce these prints.

Contents

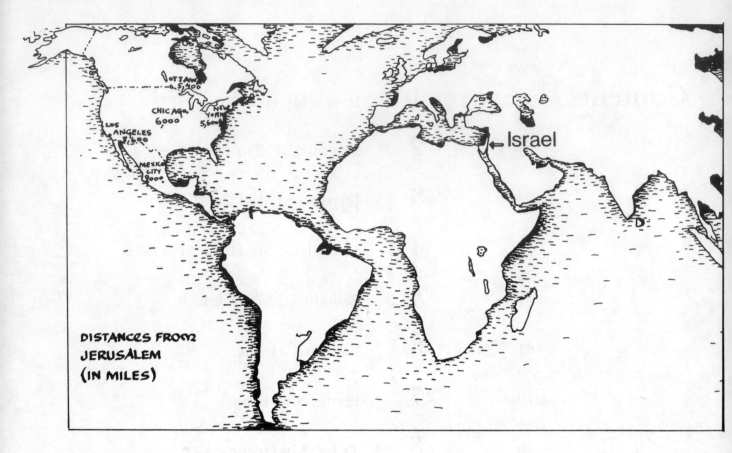

OTTAWA
5,400

CHICAGO
6,000

NEW
YORK
5,600

LOS
ANGELES
7,500

MEXICO
CITY
8,000

Israel

DISTANCES FROM
JERUSALEM
(IN MILES)

1

ISRAEL, MY HOME

TO JEWISH PEOPLE, Israel is the closest far away place in the whole wide world.

It is far away because it is 6,000 miles from the U.S.A., and it is close because it is in the hearts of Jews everywhere. It is a very

9

יִשְׂרָאֵל!

beautiful land across the ocean, and many, many Jewish people live there.

Any Jew can become a citizen of Israel; Israel is the Jewish State. If you are Jewish, you could become a citizen of Israel, too.

If you were a Jewish citizen of Israel, you would probably use some special words to tell about your home. Words like beautiful, hot, Jewish homeland, small, important, holy, historic, strong, brave, would be just a few. You would be proud to be a citizen of Israel.

Living in Israel would be very different from living in America. This book will tell you about some of those differences.

If you lived on a kibbutz . . . .

10

THIS IS ISRAEL

Here is a map of Israel. Soon you will be meeting children who live there.

Where do you think you would like to live in Israel? Draw an "X" on the place you have chosen.

Color the Negev orange.
Color the Galilee green.
Color the seas blue.

ISRAEL

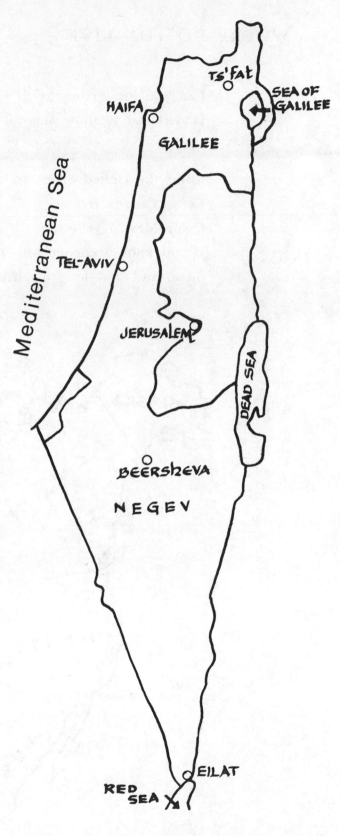

11

WHERE DO YOU LIVE?

Can you locate the city in which you live, on this map?
Draw a star to show where it is, and write the name of the city next to the star.

Color the United States and Alaska green.
Color Canada red.
Color Mexico yellow.
If you know someone who has visited Israel, find out how they traveled there, and how long the trip took.

IMPORTANT WORDS

To find four important words —
Color every box that has the number "1" blue.
Color every box that has the number "2" green.
Color every box that has the number "3" yellow.
Color every box that has the number "4" orange.

Write the four words here.

_____ _____ _____ _____

KIBBUTZ, MY HOME

SHALOM! My name is Yosi and I live on a kibbutz in the Galilee. That is the northern part of Israel. In Hebrew we call it **hagalil**.

שָׁלוֹם!

My parents, Shmuel and Sarah, were born in a town in Russia called Bialystock. They came to Israel long ago, even before Israel became a State in 1948. They like living on a kibbutz and I do too.

You might think it's strange, but nothing I have really belongs to me. Everything on a kibbutz belongs to all of us together. So you could also say, everything belongs to me! The kibbutz (which is all of us) gives us clothing, food, a place to live, and work to do, and it takes care of us when we are sick.

Instead of paying for the things we get, our job is to take care of the kibbutz by working. Our kibbutz is like a farm, and all the people who live here must do some kind of work. My father picks fruit in the orchards and puts it into large wooden crates. Other kibbutzniks load the crates onto trailers so that large

14

Fresh eggs are collected every day.

tractors can pull them to market. We also have cows and chickens and turkeys.

My mother does lots of different jobs. In the harvest season, she helps pick fruit. Sometimes she works in the kitchen preparing food for all the people on the kibbutz, and other times she works in the children's houses.

That's right. The children live together. Our children's houses are happy places, and we live in them when we are little. Because our parents all work, every day, except for Shabbat, kind, helpful people care for us and keep us busy and happy. My mother and father spend time with me every afternoon, when

15

We take care of the animals in our children's zoo.

they are finished working. And they always come to the children's house to kiss me good night.

This is the dining room in the children's house.

While my parents work and I am at the children's house, I study and I play. I have learned to read and write and spell. I also know how to do work in my math book. I study very hard, but even study can be fun because everyone in my class studies together. We don't have tests in the kibbutz school!

I also help care for the animals in our children's zoo. When I am a little older, I will spend part of each day working in the vegetable garden with the other children.

קיבוץ

On Shabbat I spend the whole day with my family. Sometimes we have a picnic with some cousins who live on another kibbutz

The older children eat in the big kibbutz dining room.

17

nearby. Other times we just stay near my parents' cottage and play silly word games, backgammon, checkers, or dominoes. In the afternoon, my mother serves us cake with sugary icing. I eat two pieces before I am full, and then I lick the sticky white sugar off my fingers.

I love our kibbutz, and I especially love to ride on the tractor when my father is driving it.

The kibbutz is the only place I would ever want to live, unless I could live in Jerusalem....

We spend a lot of time deciding what to do after school.

A WAGON OF WORDS

Yosi's father is driving a tractor that is pulling a wagon filled with letters. There are 13 words hidden in these letters. How many of them can you find?

Read across in both directions, up and down, and diagonally. Circle each word you find.

```
F  S  H  A  B  B  A  T
Y  Z  L  F  R  U  I  T
S  T  R  A  C  T  O  R
H  U  O  M  E  N  Q  U
A  B  E  I  E  B  L  S
L  B  D  L  O  N  R  S
O  I  I  Y  O  S  I  I
M  K  R  O  W  S  G  A
```

Did you find all these words?   work   tractor   Russia   fruit
family   kibbutz   Yosi   men   boy   girl   ride   Shabbat
shalom

19

ON THE KIBBUTZ

Can you help Yosi get to the barn so that he can feed the cows? Be sure not to cross over any fences!

20

WHAT DO YOU THINK?

Here's a chance to make a list of some of the things you would find different, if you were to live on a kibbutz.

_____

_____

_____

_____

_____

Make a check √ next to each difference that you think you would enjoy.

Make a question mark ? next to each difference that you think you might not enjoy.

Compare your answers with your friends' answers.

21

A KIBBUTZ
CROSSWORD PUZZLE

Down

1 Galilee is the name of the _____ part of Israel.

2 The kibbutz is _____ for Yosi.

3 On a kibbutz, everyone must _____ .

6 _____ became a state in 1948.

7 Some animals live in a _____ .

9 Shabbat is a day of _____ .

Across

3 Men and _____ work on a kibbutz.

4 Father and _____ come to the children's house to say goodnight.

5 Yosi lives on a _____ .

8 Vegetables, cows and chickens are raised on a _____ .

10 The kibbutz takes _____ of everyone who lives on it.

11 The Hebrew name for Galilee is _____ .

You can check your answers on p. 127.

I LIVE IN ISRAEL

JERUSALEM, MY HOME

PART ONE

אִמָּא

MY NAME is Avi. I have three big sisters. My parent's names are Esther and Dov, but I call them **Imma** and **Abba**. We all live in the city of Jerusalem.

אַבָּא

Jerusalem is the capital of the State of Israel and is known by many people as "The Holy City." It is holy to the Moslems and the Christians, as well as to the Jews. You can tell that Jerusalem is important to so many different people just by walking through it.

Some of Jerusalem is very old and is surrounded by a high stone wall. That part is called the Old City. In the Old City you can see Jews praying at the Western Wall, and Moslems praying in their mosques. Christians walk along the crowded, narrow streets in the Old City on their way to the different churches. In Jerusalem, Jews and Arabs work together every single day.

But part of Jerusalem is very modern. That's where our family lives. Our house is made of Jerusalem stone.

23

Cars are not allowed in the Old City, so donkeys carry all the goods.

Some people live in the New City and work in the Old City, or the other way around! It is exciting to live in Jerusalem which is so old and so new at the same time. I live in a modern apartment house, but from my window I can see the hill where King Solomon built the Temple that we read about in the Bible.

I am in the second grade, and we learn about Jerusalem and the history of the Jews in school. Of course, all our classes are in Hebrew, because that is the language of Israel. It's easy to learn history in Jerusalem, because it is all around us. When our class goes to the Israel Museum, we see 2,000 year old Dead Sea Scrolls in the Shrine of the Book; then we look at modern sculp-

tures in the museum's garden. In Jerusalem, automobiles and donkey carts travel on the same street.

I have learned that people thought Jerusalem was important for a very long time — long, long before my great-grandfather came here.

Many cities are important because they are near the water, and boats can bring travelers and cargo there from far-away places. But Jerusalem is not very close to the Mediterranean Sea, where I love to swim and jump in the waves. It is not close to the Red Sea or the Sea of Galilee. Even the closest sea, the Dead Sea, is several miles away. Actually, Jerusalem is right in the very middle of Israel, on top of a mountain.

People of many religions live together in Jerusalem.

25

Jerusalem is important because it is the capital of Israel. The President of Israel lives here. The Government of Israel meets here. The Knesset in Jerusalem is the building where the Prime Minister and the representatives of Israel's political parties meet to decide the best way to run the country. Although the Knesset members disagree sometimes, they all want what is best for Israel.

Jerusalem is important for other reasons, too. My father says that without Jerusalem, there would be no State of Israel today.

A very long time ago, King David made Jerusalem his capital city; then it was called "The City of David." The king wanted to

David's Citadel helped protect Jerusalem.

I LIVE IN ISRAEL

This is the Knesset building.

build a beautiful Temple in Jerusalem where the Ark of the Law could be kept. Inside the Ark of the Law were the two stone tablets that Moses had brought down from Mount Sinai. But King David never built the Temple. He was too busy fighting wars to keep his kingdom safe.

It was David's son, King Solomon, who built the First Temple in Jerusalem. In Solomon's time, the kingdom of Israel was at peace. King Solomon chose the highest and most beautiful spot

27

Here is the home of the President of Israel.

This is one of the seven gates in the Old City wall.

in the city for the Temple. People from all over Israel came to pray there, and Jerusalem became the Holy City for the Jews. Later, prophets like Isaiah and Jeremiah spoke to the people in Jerusalem, warning them to stop doing evil. The prophets tried to help the people learn to do only good things.

The Temple is gone now, but today, no matter where Jews live, we still turn toward Jerusalem when we pray. And we can visit the spot where the Temple used to stand, in the Old City of Jerusalem.

Sometimes I go to the Old City with my mother and sisters. The Old City is surrounded by a high stone wall. We have to pass through a tall gate to get in. That is how cities were protected long, long ago. Inside the Old City the streets are very narrow. They are full of people and very noisy. And from time to time everyone has to squeeze against the walls, so a donkey loaded with groceries or pottery can pass through the narrow street.

Red and green and purple vegetables are piled outside the tiny shops, and meat hangs from big hooks inside. We smell the fresh bread and look hungrily into the shops until my mother buys each of us a treat — a **pita**, a flat Arab bread covered with sesame seeds.

When we hear the sound of hammering, we know that our old friend Uri is busy working. Uri is a coppersmith. He came to

29

There's a lot to see in the Old City.

יְרוּשָׁלַיִם

Jerusalem from Yemen, where his father and his grandfather and his great-grandfather were coppersmiths. Jews have come from a hundred countries to live in Jerusalem. I like watching Uri as he hammers beautiful pictures and designs on pieces of copper. At home we have a large copper tray that Uri made; on it is a picture of the Old City of Jerusalem, and its name in Hebrew — **Ye-ru-sha-la-yim.**

You have to climb a hill to get to the place where the Temple used to stand. It is called the Temple Mount. It is very quiet up

30

there, and the sounds of the city seem far away. On the hill is a beautiful building that is holy to the Moslems. It is called the Dome of the Rock. People who want to go in have to take their shoes off before they enter. Moslems feel that it is a sign of respect to remove one's shoes before entering a holy place.

Inside, I climbed down some stairs and touched the rock where Abraham took Isaac and bound him for a sacrifice. Finally, of course, God told Abraham to sacrifice a ram instead. All that happened long ago. My father told me the story, and then I read it in the Bible.

It was hot when we came down from the Temple Mount, and we stopped for an ice cream cone. Israel has good ice cream. I should know, for I eat a lot of it.

The Dome of the Rock stands on the Temple Mount.

Before we go home from the Old City, Mother always takes us to pray at the Western Wall. In Hebrew we call it **hakotel**, which means "the Wall." Here is what I know about the Wall.

When the First Temple was destroyed, the Jews were carried off to Babylonia. Later many Jews returned to Jerusalem, and they built a Second Temple. It was not as big as the first, but it had a strong protecting wall all around it. Then the Romans came and destroyed the Second Temple. Now the Western Wall is all that is left of the wall that protected the Temple. It is very important to us because it reminds us of the Temple of long ago.

Can you see the cracks where people hide their prayer-notes?

Jews could not always visit the Western Wall as they can today. But in 1967, many brave Israeli soldiers fought and died for Jerusalem, and now Israelis and visitors from all over the world can come to the Wall to pray. Some take pictures of it. Some cry when they stand next to it. Some write prayers on small pieces of paper and tuck the folded paper into the cracks between the stones. Nearly everyone says a prayer at the Western Wall.

In a few years, I will be Bar Mitzvah at the Wall. It is the most special place to me.

Jerusalem is filled with many other special places, but they are each special in a different way. One of these places is Mea Shearim . . .

33

WHO BUILT THE TEMPLE?

To discover the name of the king who built the First Temple in Jerusalem:

Color every stone with a dot in it, blue.

Color the other stones to finish the picture.

34

CHOOSE THE RIGHT WORD

Circle the word that best completes each sentence.

1 Jerusalem is the (port, capital, lowest) city of Israel.

2 It is located in the (west, south, middle) of the country.

3 The Knesset makes the (books, ice cream, laws) for the State.

4 Jews and (Arabs, Austrians, Australians) live and work together in Jerusalem.

5 The Old City walls were built for (warmth, disguise, protection).

6 David's son, (President, King, Prime Minister) Solomon, built the First Temple.

7 Since the Temple was destroyed, Jews all over the world turn to Jerusalem when they (play, sway, pray).

8 The prophets warned the people to stop (smoking, doing evil, making noise).

9 Jews pray in a synagogue, Christians in a church, and Moslems in a (market, mosque, motel).

10 **Hakotel** is the Hebrew word for the Western (Wall, hole, gate).

You can check your answers on p. 127. Enter your score here. _____

A MAP OF JERUSALEM

Here is a map of the city of Jerusalem.

Color the Old City yellow.
Color the New City green.
Decorate your map.
Here is a list of some places in Jerusalem that you've read about.
Next to each one, write an "O" if it is in the Old City, and an "N" if it is in the New City.

Western Wall _____   market place _____

Knesset _____   President's House _____

Dome of the Rock _____   Israel Museum _____

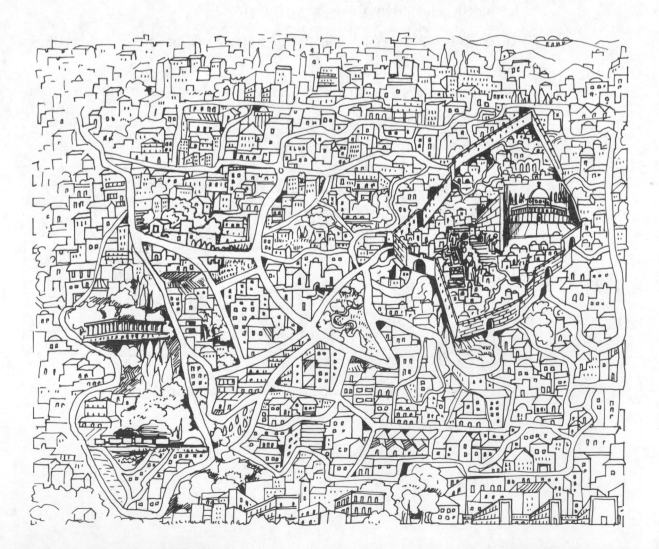

JERUSALEM, MY HOME

PART TWO

MEA SHEARIM is a neighborhood in Jerusalem where many Orthodox Jews live.

My mother calls it a **shtetl** — that is what the small Jewish towns in Europe were called a hundred years ago. She says that going to Mea Shearim is like turning the clock back one hundred years.

My friend Moshe lives in Mea Shearim. We like to visit him and his family. Although Moshe's family knows Hebrew, they and all their neighbors speak Yiddish among themselves, for they believe that Hebrew is the holy language of the Bible and should be used only for prayers and study. Moshe doesn't call his parents **Imma** and **Abba**, the way I do. He calls them **Mammeh** and **Tatteh**.

Moshe is learning to follow all the laws of the Torah and Talmud very carefully. He tries to say his prayers three times a day along with his father, but he cannot pray as fast yet, for he does not know the prayers as well as his father does.

37

The children in Mea Shearim study very hard.

Moshe and his father.

Moshe goes to school in a yeshiva in Mea Shearim. He studies all the subjects that I do, and more! He learns how to read, write and do arithmetic, and he also studies the Bible, Jewish history, laws and prayers. He will know a lot by the time he grows up.

Moshe's father and brothers wear large round black hats and long black coats. Moshe wears a small round black hat and a

I LIVE IN ISRAEL

small black coat. He looks very important dressed that way. Moshe has **payot**, long curls of hair on each side of his face. He says that Orthodox men and boys never cut this hair because the Torah commandments tell them not to.

Moshe's mother wears a scarf or wig over her hair. She has done this since she was married. Moshe's sister, Leah, will also cover her hair when she grows up and gets married. Leah and her mother always wear dresses with long sleeves, and long stockings, even when it is very hot in the summer. They say that a woman should dress modestly.

When I visit my friend on Shabbat, I feel that I am in another part of the world. Shabbat with Moshe is perfect.

Jumping rope is fun, wherever you live.

39

Before Shabbat, Moshe's mother and sister work very hard to prepare a delicious meal. Dinner is warm and spicy and filling. After dinner everyone sings and sings. On Shabbat we sing special songs called **z'mirot**. I know some of the songs, but Moshe knows more. I know many of the prayers, too, but Moshe knows more prayers than I do.

We walk to the beautiful synagogue the next day, and try to pray as well as everyone else. The **bima** is round, and the carved wooden Ark which holds the Torah is round, too. I don't go home until after Havdalah services in the evening. I hope someday Moshe will spend Shabbat with my family and me. Then I can take him to our synagogue and show him our holy Torah.

שַׁבָּת שָׁלוֹם!

Here is a sukkah in Mea Shearim.

Sometimes I think everything about Jerusalem is holy! There are lots of places in Jerusalem that remind you of people and stories of the Bible. We invited Moshe to visit some of these places with us when there was a school vacation. We all got into our car and drove down a long winding road to see Zachariah's tomb and the tomb of Absalom. Zachariah was a prophet, and Absalom was one of the sons of King David. Next year I will learn about them in school.

When we stopped to visit the tombs, my father reminded me to watch out for the wiggly caterpillars he called centipedes. He

41

told me they are called centipedes because they have a hundred legs, but I should not stop to count them, because they might sting me.

After we left the tombs, we drove past Hezekiah's tunnel. I love the tunnel. It's long and dark, and there is water at the bottom of it. Walking through it is always so scary.

Once I waded through the tunnel with Uri the coppersmith. We held candles to light our way. Uri told me that long ago, in the time of the Kings of Israel, this was a very secret tunnel that brought drinking water into the city of Jerusalem. I felt very important when I shared this secret with my class at school. Of course, I didn't tell them I was scared when I was in the tunnel, or that I held very tightly to Uri's hand when the water reached almost to my chin!

Yad Absalom was named after King David's son.

Zachariah's Tomb was carved out of a rocky hillside

The Museum collects costumes that were worn by Jews all over the world.
We tried on some of them!

Next we drove to the Israel Museum. My favorite exhibit in the museum is the very old **sukkah**. It is the oldest **sukkah** I have ever seen. Its walls are of wood, painted with beautiful fruits and flowers. Moshe and I wished we could eat in it during Sukkot.

The Israel Museum also has collections of beautiful costumes of Jews from many lands. When I look at them, I wish I could try them on. There are many ancient jars and containers made of clay and stone, discovered by archaeologists who dig in the ground all over Israel to find out how people used to live long, long ago. These jars and bowls were used by Jews who lived here thousands of years ago, and now we can see them right before

43

Our school, planting trees on Tu B'Shevat.

The Hanukkah menorahs in the Israel Museum come from many different lands.

Sometimes we play "statues" in the sculpture garden of the Museum.

our eyes! The Israel Museum has collections of coins and Torahs, pictures and menorahs. There are so many things in the museum that I know I will have to visit it many times before I will be able to see them all.

My father says that the next time we visit special places in Jerusalem we will go to a different kind of museum. It is called Yad Vashem and it is a memorial to all the Jewish people who were killed in Europe during the Holocaust.

We ended our trip at the Jerusalem Forest. We all sat under the trees and had a wonderful picnic. I told Moshe that on Tu

45

B'Shevat our class goes to the forest to plant trees. Trees are very important to our country, for without them the hot sun would bake the earth and nothing would grow. Trees give us shade and help protect the plants that grow beneath them. They also give us wood for making chairs, desks, tables and paper. Even before there was a State of Israel, the Jewish National Fund began to plant trees and forests here.

After such a long trip, Moshe and I were both very tired. As we drove back to the city, I stared out the window of the car and dreamed about what it would be like if I lived somewhere else.

My life would be so different if I lived in Beersheva . . .

אִם גָּרְתִּי

date palm   olive   oak   eucalyptus

IN THE JERUSALEM FOREST

Hidden in this picture of the Jerusalem Forest are four different kinds of trees — olive, date palm, oak and eucalyptus

Can you find them? Color them green. Then color the rest of the picture.

JERUSALEM CROSSWORD PUZZLE

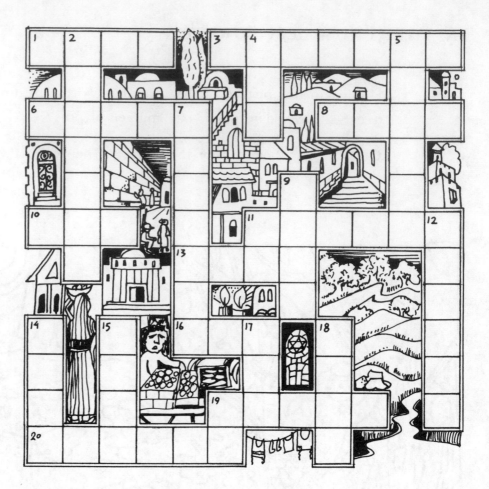

Across

1 This protected the ancient Temple

3 A part of Jerusalem surrounded by a wall

6 We plant these on Tu B'Shevat

8 Jerusalem, My _____

10 _____ Vashem is a memorial museum

11 Jerusalem is holy to the Jew, the Christian and the _____

13 Something you eat three times a day

16 The _____ City is the modern part of Jerusalem

19 Abraham's son

20 Many shade trees grow in a _____

48

Down

2 The first Jew

4 The Ark of the _____ was placed in Solomon's Temple

5 In the time of the Bible, Jews came to the _____ to pray

7 King David's son

9 Three religions call Jerusalem the _____ City

11 Short for Mother

12 There are interesting collections in the Israel _____

14 First letter of the Hebrew alphabet

15 **Payot** are long curls of _____

17 Today it **is**; yesterday it _____

18 Jerusalem is not _____ any sea, but far from water

19 You are _____! (game)

You will find the solution on p. 127.

49

JERUSALEM IN STAMPS

Here are pictures of some postage stamps from Israel. They show special places in the city of Jerusalem.

Can you identify some of the places shown on each stamp? Write them below each picture.

Now, choose one stamp and write a short story or a poem about the place shown on it.

5

BEERSHEVA, MY HOME

בְּאֵר שֶׁבַע

MY NAME is Tova and I live in Beersheva. It is the most important city in the Negev. The Negev is the southern part of Israel.

I live with my mother and my Uncle Menahem. My father is dead. He was one of the soldiers killed in the Yom Kippur War. My mother's name is Rivka. She works part-time at the University, teaching students modern farming methods and ways to raise better crops.

We live in a third-floor apartment. In Israel, we do not rent apartments; instead, we buy them, just like American families buy homes. There are no elevators in our apartment building, and we are used to going up and down the stairs without huffing and puffing.

We are also used to walking to the store for anything we need. No one in our family has a car, and we carry all our groceries back from the store by ourselves. We do not mind. My mother says that all the exercise makes us very strong.

51

It is very cool in our school, even on hot days.

Most of the year Beersheva is hot. We do not have any air conditioners to cool us off. Luckily, every afternoon there is a breeze that cools us off a little. But when the weather is cold, our house is heated by big frames of glass on the roof. They are called solar heating panels, because they collect heat from the sun. That heat also warms the water in our apartment. Lots of people in Israel use solar heating panels to warm our homes and to heat the water we use. That's because we have so much sunlight, especially in the Negev.

All the Negev is very hot and dry, like a desert. My mother told me that before the State of Israel was created in 1948, no one

52

lived in the Negev except Bedouins. Bedouins are nomads who live in tents and move about the desert with their flocks of sheep and goats. My mother also explained that nothing used to grow in the Negev, because there was no water. But now there are great big pipes that carry precious water all the way from the Sea of Galilee in the north, down to the Negev.

Now people live in the Negev, and many crops grow here. The water that is piped in, is used to irrigate the fields.

There are still many Bedouins living in the Negev. Near our apartment there is a marketplace. Every Thursday I see the Bedouins bringing their camels and goats and sheep to market

All the roofs have solar heaters.

Here is a Bedouin camp.

In the Negev, the camel-rider knows the way best.

54

to sell. I have a Bedouin friend who often comes to the city with her family on market day. During the summer vacation we play together in the morning while her father sells and trades.

My friend's name is Dulah, and she is very nice. Dulah does not have to go to school at all. She lives just outside of the city, in a tent, with her family. Her family's goats live in the tent, too. I do not think I would like goats living in our apartment with my mother and uncle. I do not think they would like it either.

Dulah showed me how to milk a goat and drink the warm milk. At first, I did not like it because it does not taste like cow's milk.

Market-day in Beersheva.

BEERSHEVA, MY HOME

It is heavier and thicker. But the more I drink it, the more I like the thick, warm taste in my mouth.

Dulah wears a ring in her nose and told me that most Bedouin girls wear nose-rings. I told her it looks very nice, but I am glad that I do not wear one. Dulah tells me the Arabic name for lots of things, and I tell her the name in Hebrew. We play for a few hours until her father calls, and it is time for her to return to her tent in the desert.

When Dulah leaves, it is also time for me to return to our apartment so that my mother will not worry. Before Dulah goes, she

Going home from the market.

56

This is what Abraham's Well looks like now.　　These huge pipes carry water to the Negev.

shares a piece of dried fruit with me. It tastes like sugared apricots, and is so thin from being rolled flat, that at first I think it is a piece of leather. It is delicious, and I wish I had an extra piece.

On the way home, I go past Abraham's Well. The Bible tells us that Abraham owned this well. He used to draw water from it to drink and to give to his sheep, thousands of years ago.

Next week, my Uncle Menachem will be on vacation from his job, and he promised to take me on a bus ride to see the beautiful fish in the Red Sea. If I lived in Eilat . . .

57

ABRAHAM'S WELL

Abraham, the first Jew, lived 4,000 years ago. When he was young, he took care of his father's idols. When he grew up, he believed in the one God.

Abraham was a shepherd. He bought this well so he could give water to his sheep and goats in the fields. Today the well stands in the modern city of Beersheva.

As you can see, ten stones are missing from Abraham's Well. Answer the questions below, and check your answers on p. 127. For each correct answer, you can color in one stone.

1 Whose well are you repairing? _____

2 How old is it? _____

3 What is it made of? _____

4 Who drank from it long ago? _____

5 Where was the well when Abraham bought it? _____

_____

6 Where is the well today? _____

7 Who was Abraham? _____

_____

8 What did Abraham take care of when he was a child? _____

_____

9 Whom did he believe in when he was grown up? _____

10 Do you know the name of Abraham's son? _____

58

FOLLOWING THE PIPELINE

The pipes that carry water from the Sea of Galilee to the Negev bring water to many farms and villages, towns and cities in Israel. They are mostly underground, and you cannot see them. But if you can find your way through this maze, you will see how long the pipe line is.

Use a colored pencil or a crayon to show the way.

59

A LETTER FROM BEERSHEVA

Write a letter to a friend, telling all you can about Beersheva and its people.

Dear _____ ,

_____

_____

_____

_____

_____

_____

Love,

_____

60

6

EILAT, MY HOME

אֵילַת

MY NAME is Saul and I live in Eilat. Eilat is the most southern city in Israel. It is on the shore of the Red Sea.

My brother, Dan, takes care of me because my parents died when I was little. Dan is a fisherman. He goes out in a boat early every morning to catch fish in the Red Sea. When he comes back, he cleans the fish and sells them. They are shipped all over Israel. It is nice to know that some of the fish that Israelis eat come from the catches that Dan brings in each day.

When Dan and I first came to Eilat from Morocco, I did not think I would like it here, but now I wouldn't want to live anywhere else. The weather is hot the year round and it hardly ever rains. We even go swimming in the winter. Sometimes, after school is over and Dan is finished fishing, we go snorkeling in the Red Sea. The sea has the clearest, bluest water you could ever imagine. I asked Dan why it is called the Red Sea, when the water is so blue. He told me I would find out late in the afternoon. I thought that was a strange answer. But then I saw that

61

when the sun began to set, the mountains around the Red Sea turned red and purple. They were reflected in the clear water of the sea, and that seemed to turn red, too!

Under the water there are so many different colored fish that it seems as if rainbows are swimming by. The fish are speckled and striped and silvery and bronze. Some are big and fat; others, long and skinny. Some are tiny as can be. Sometimes we take a ride in a glass-bottomed boat. Through the glass, the sea is as colorful as a Purim carnival, and we can see the coral reef looking like an undersea flower garden.

If this picture were in color, you would see how beautiful the coral reef is!

62

Mending nets is an important part of a fisherman's work.

Lots of hands are needed to pull in the fishing nets.

For a special treat, Dan takes me to the Marine Observatory. That is a very special kind of museum that is under-water. We walk along a high boardwalk far out over the sea. Then we go into a building and down a long flight of stairs. At the bottom of the stairs we are in a round room with big windows. When we look out, we are under the sea and the fish are swimming by, right past our noses! Some seem to look right at us. Others hide behind the waving sea plants.

These beautiful fish and the coral reef are part of an Underwater Nature Reserve. That means that they are protected by law. We

63

EILAT, MY HOME

Notice how close the mountains are to the sea.

are not allowed to pick the coral and plants, or catch the fish. Dan only catches the fish outside the Nature Reserve, and only the ones that are good to eat.

But Eilat is more than just a good place to watch and catch fish. It is Israel's most southern port. Ships come from all over the world, bringing goods to be unloaded in Eilat. Many oil tankers dock here. Some of the oil is stored in big tanks, and some is sent to other places in Israel in huge oil pipelines. The docks

64

and the tanks don't smell very good. I always hold my nose as we go by.

Eilat is also a resort city. Lots of Israelis come here for their vacation. They stay at hotels, and they swim and snorkel in the clear waters of the Red Sea. In the winter, tourists come from countries where it is cold and snowy. When they return to their homes, they are sunburned! Some visitors come to Eilat by car or bus; it is a very long drive. So some people fly down to Eilat, from Tel Aviv or Jerusalem.

The hotels in Eilat are right on the beach.

EILAT, MY HOME

Coming in for a landing at Eilat!

The last time I was at the airport, my brother Dan and I went to say goodbye to my friend Aliza. Aliza used to live in Eilat, but she moved with her parents to Haifa. Haifa is also a port city, like Eilat, but it is much bigger and not as warm. Haifa is in the north, on the Mediterranean Sea with its cool sea breezes.

If I lived in Haifa, imagine what that would be like . . .

66

THE MARINE OBSERVATORY

To see what is outside the window, connect the dots.

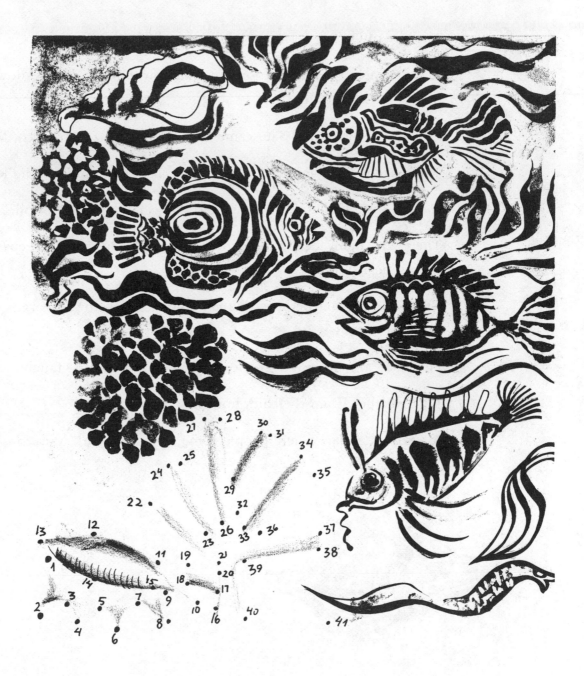

EILAT, MY HOME

A LOT ABOUT EILAT

Circle the correct words in each sentence. You can check your answers on p. 127.

1 The city of (Ts'fat, Tel Aviv, Eilat) is on the Red Sea.

2 Many Israelis spend vacations in Eilat (swimming, sliding down sand dunes, picking fruit).

3 Our story tells us that Saul came from (Puerto Rico, Morocco, Maine).

4 There are many colored (ribbons, rocks, fish) swimming in the Red Sea.

5 A tanker is a (balloon, ship, market) that carries a cargo of oil.

6 There are many beautiful (coral reefs, curly sheep, oily jeeps) in the waters near Eilat.

7 Eilat is important because (planes, ships, cars) bring in cargo from all over the world.

8 Fish that are protected are forbidden to be (caught, taught, bought).

9 Eilat weather is mostly (cold, hot, rainy).

10 A resort is a place where people come to (study, work, vacation).

HIDDEN TREASURE

One day Saul and Dan went out in a glass-bottomed boat. To their surprise, among the fish on the coral reef, they saw a treasure chest. In it they found lots of letters. Hidden among them were 13 words. Can you find them? They all appear in the story about Eilat.

Read across, down, and diagonally. Circle the words when you find them.

Did you find all these words?

Red Sea Eilat ship tanker port reef fish resort hot sun oil airport coral

EILAT, MY HOME

HAIFA, MY HOME

MY NAME is Aliza. I live with my mother in Haifa. My father is an officer in the army, but he comes to Haifa to be with us whenever he can. My mother is a chemistry teacher at the Technion. That is a university that trains engineers and architects.

I think Haifa is the most beautiful city in all Israel. Others must have thought so, too, for the name Haifa means "beautiful coast." The city is shaped like the letter "C". In the opening of the "C" is a large harbor. Big ships from all over the world come to Haifa's harbor. They pick up and deliver everything that keeps the large factories and refineries busy.

אוֹלִים

The ships also bring new **olim** to Israel. **Olim** is what we call newcomers who have decided to settle in Israel. We are always very happy to have new Jewish settlers come to our land to live.

My family is very lucky, for we live in our own house in Haifa. It is half-way up a sloping hill which is part of the Mount Carmel mountains. We can see the lovely Mediterranean Sea by

70

daylight and at night we look over all the twinkling lights of the city. There are lots of them.

חֵיפָה

Though there are beautiful flowers everywhere in Israel, I think that Haifa has more than any other place. They grow in our small garden, and in front of the stores. They are in the parks and they are near the edges of the streets. They even grow beside the school yards. I go to the Leo Baeck School, and there are flowers in our school courtyard.

I can see Haifa Bay from my window.

HAIFA, MY HOME

My school is on the slope of Mount Carmel, just like my house. It is large and cool. My teachers are very nice, but they give me lots of hard school-work. I go to school six days a week.

When there is no school, I sometimes walk down to the beach with my mother. Sometimes my father is able to join us. When he is with us, we play paddle-ball. We each hold a paddle and hit a ball back and forth with it. When we are tired, Mother gives us lunch. We have hard-boiled eggs, tomatoes, creamy yogurt, bread and cheese for lunch. Some days we buy frozen ices on a stick for dessert.

When we visit the beach, I like to look at the new hotel being built for the tourists. It is the second time the builders have built

Everyone in the family enjoys the seashore.

Here is the old hotel that sank, and the new one alongside it.

it. The first time, they had the wide side facing the water. When it was almost finished, it began to sink in the sand! The builders had to start all over again, but this time they turned it sideways and it did not sink. My American cousins would not believe this story, but it is true!

Once, my father took me on a bus to a town near Haifa. It is very old and it used to be called Acre. We call it Akko. It is an Arab town, but many Jews live there too. Akko is an interesting city to visit. I saw a tall mosque with an ancient sundial in front of it. The letters were written in Turkish, and though I could not

עכו

73

HAIFA, MY HOME

Jews and Arabs come to the marketplace
to buy and to talk.

This is the Khan in Akko — where
the camel caravans used to spend the night.

understand what was written, I told my father that I thought it
was three o'clock. Father smiled at me when I pretended to read
the sundial.

The Arab markets in Akko remind me of the market I visited in
the Old City of Jerusalem. The streets are narrow and lined with
rows of shops. There is a spicy smell in the air. There are no
supermarkets in Akko, but lots of little stores, each selling just
one kind of food — cakes, or cheeses, vegetables, or meat; even
stores that only sell spices, coffee beans and nuts. Some stores

74

sell live chickens and some sell live rabbits. There are restaurants and snack bars and barber shops. And there are stores that just sell jackets made out of sheepskin. It is always fun to visit the Arab markets.

As we rode on the bus back to Haifa, I thought of the holiday that was coming soon, Rosh Hashanah. We would be going to Ts'fat for the holiday, to stay with Aunt Rosa and Uncle Yosef. I'm glad that I'll get to play with my cousin Ettie. We always bake dozens of honey cookies, play hopscotch, and listen to ghost stories on her record player. How I like to visit Ts'fat . . .

Pita is delicious, especially when it's hot from the oven.

75

ISRAELI COINS

Because Haifa is a harbor, sailors come there from all over the world. One sailor had all these coins in his pocket. Can you tell the Israeli coins from all the others? Color the Israeli coins yellow.

I LIVE IN ISRAEL

SHIP OF WORDS

This ship is arriving at Haifa with a cargo of hidden words. Can you find them? Look across in both directions, up and down, and diagonally. Circle the words when you find them.

```
M E D I T E R R A N E A N
H A I F A F Q H K U H S E
A P R N F D C I K B P H W
R T I K M J Z L O I R A C
B X N C E B E L H A O B O
O T R C I T Y S F L N B M
R U N I V E R S I T Y A E
I C E C R E A M P T I T R
I S R A E L F L O W E R S
```

Did you find all these words?

Haifa   harbor   university   ships   Israel   hills   Mediterranean
flowers   city   Shabbat   ice cream   Akko   market   newcomers   shuk

WELCOME!

These **olim** (newcomers) have just arrived in Haifa. Their families and friends have come to welcome them.

Connect the dots and you will find out how they arrived in Israel.

Imagine you have just arrived in Haifa. Your Aunt Shosh and Uncle Benny have come to meet you. Can you imagine what you might say to one another? Can you continue this dialogue?

Aunt Shosh: **Shalom** _____ (your name). Welcome to Israel.
                 Baruch haba!
_____ : **Shalom,** Aunt Shosh!
Uncle Benny: **Shalom, shalom,** we're very happy you've come to Israel.
                 There are many things we want to show you.

_____ : _____

_____

_____

_____

_____

_____

_____

שָׁלוֹם! בָּרוּק הַבָּא!

בְּרוּכָה הַבָּאָה!

79

8

TS'FAT, MY HOME

MY NAME is Ettie and I live in Ts'fat with my mother, Rosa, my father, Yosef, and my five brothers and sisters. My family came from Bulgaria, but I was born in Israel. I am a **sabra**.

Whenever someone is born in Israel we call that person a **sabra**. Sabra is the fruit of the cactus, and it is hard and prickly on the outside, but very sweet on the inside. People say that when you are born in Israel, you are like that, too.

צֶפֶת

צָפוֹ

Ts'fat is perched high on the side of a mountain. It is the main city in Upper Galilee, the northern part of Israel. On a clear day, we can see far across the green countryside all around. My sister P'nina and I like to stand on our porch trying to count the sparkles dancing on the Sea of Galilee in the distance. The name Ts'fat comes from the Hebrew word **tsafo** which means "lookout." It is a perfect name for my city.

A long time ago, in the days of the Second Temple, the people of Ts'fat lit bonfires on the top of our mountain to signal to

80

people in far-away towns and villages the beginning of a new month or a festival.

Many years later, a group of people called mystics came and settled in Ts'fat. They were called mystics because they believed they knew certain secrets or mysteries about God and the world which others did not know. They wrote many prayers that we still recite. Their leader was a great rabbi called **Ha-Ari**, "The

This picture shows why Ts'fat got its name!

This is what a *sabra* looks like in a garden.

Sometimes the artists draw
the children who live in Ts'fat.

Lion." He was wise, kind and understanding, strong and brave.
People loved him and used to come to Ts'fat to study with him.

Now, people come here for other reasons. Many come to live in
Ts'fat for their health. My mother says that the clean, dry mountain air is very good for us. Painters and sculptors have come to
live here, too. They like the bright sunshine and the beautiful
hilly countryside. Many of their pictures are of the mountains
and the city, and the people who live here. They do such fine

82

בֵּית כְּנֶסֶת
הָאֲרִי

The Ari Synagogue has a beautiful Ark for the Torah scrolls.

work that tourists often come to Ts'fat just to buy pictures. They take them back to hang in their homes and synagogues. Many of the artists live in a special part of Ts'fat called the Artists-Quarter.

Ts'fat is also famous for its many synagogues. They are very old. My family and I have a favorite synagogue where we go on the Holy Days. Mama, my sisters, and I sit upstairs to pray, while Papa and my brothers sit downstairs.

83

What I like most is walking past "Sefardi's" Music Store. Sefardi is a very old man who carves musical instruments out of wood. We like to stand in the soft wood shavings on the floor and watch him work with his two knives. Sometimes he tests the instruments by blowing through them, or by strumming strings he attaches to them. We hear him sing folk songs which I do not know. Papa says he is singing in Ladino. That is a mixture of Spanish and Hebrew.

Sefardi reminds me of my cousin Gershon. Gershon plays the flute and the guitar. When he comes to visit us, he brings the flute and plays it. But I'd rather visit Gershon in his home in Tel Aviv. Maybe some day I'll live in Tel Aviv....

There's not much traffic, so we can play in the street.

THE SABBATH QUEEN

One of the prayers that the mystics wrote in Ts'fat is **Lecha Dodi**. It tells that the Sabbath Queen is coming, and that we all go out to greet her. The mystics would go out into the fields around Ts'fat on Friday afternoon, and as the sun set behind the mountains, they would sing this poem-prayer.

We sing **Lecha Dodi** in the synagogue every Friday night.

Use this space to draw a picture showing how the mystics welcomed the Sabbath Queen. Or, draw a picture showing how **you** welcome the Sabbath Queen.

85

WHAT IS EGGED?

Every Israeli knows that the best way to get from town to town in Israel is by "Egged." But you may not know what Egged is.
To find out, connect the dots in the picture below.

Sometimes Egged rides are very long. To pass the time, Ettie wrote this poem.

Any place you want to go
The Egged bus will take you;
Sometimes fast — and sometimes slow,
The ride will always shake you.

Can you write a poem about riding on an Egged bus? You can begin with this line:

An Egged bus is a lot of fun

_____

_____

_____

87

ALL ABOUT TS'FAT

You can write a story about Ts'fat by filling in the blanks. There is a one-letter clue in each missing word to help you.

1 Ts'fat is the main town of the Upper __ a __ __ __ __ __

2 Ts'fat is built high on a __ __ u __ __ __ __ __

3 The Hebrew word **tsafo** means __ __ o __ ⁻ o __ __

4 The pure mountain air is good for your __ __ __ l __ __

5 Long ago, festivals began when people near Ts'fat saw the
b __ __ __ __ __ __ __ on the mountain top.

6 A famous and wise rabbi who lived in Ts'fat long ago was called
Ha-Ari, which means The __ __ __ n

7 Many __ r __ __ __ __ __ that we recite in the synagogue were
written by the rabbis in Ts'fat hundreds of years ago.

8 There are many old __ y __ __ __ __ __ __ __ __ in Ts'fat.

9 Tourists come to buy pictures from the __ __ t __ __ __ __

10 A person born in Israel is called a s __ __ __ __

11 The language that is a mixture of Spanish and Hebrew is
l __ __ __ __

You can check your answers on p. 127.

88

TEL AVIV, MY HOME

תֵּל אָבִיב

MY NAME is Gershon and I live in Tel Aviv. It is the largest city in Israel. I live here with my parents, Litza and Zalman, and my sisters. We love Tel Aviv because it is so busy. People are always going to or from work, marketing, or visiting friends. They go to the theatres, the movies and the museums. The city is always crowded. It is a white-looking, sunny city right on the shores of the Mediterranean Sea.

Tel Aviv is a very young city. It was built on sand dunes when my grandfather was a little boy. When Tel Aviv was new, it was a suburb of Jaffa. But now, Tel Aviv is so much bigger, that we call Jaffa the suburb!

Jaffa was a small ancient port. I learned in school that when King Solomon built the Temple in Jerusalem, he sent for large cedar trees from Lebanon. They were brought by ship to the port of Jaffa. When my **Zayde** (that's what I call my grandfather) came to Israel, he got off the ship in the port of Jaffa, too.

89

This old photo shows Tel Aviv being built on the sand dunes.

My family and I like to go to Dizengoff Circle. It is named after Tel Aviv's first mayor, and is a place with stores, outdoor cafes, a park, and a sparkling fountain. On holidays, Dizengoff Circle is very crowded. Sometimes we meet friends and sit at tables outside the small restaurants. We order felafel, pita, and plates of humus and tehina. These are Arab foods, but everyone in Israel eats them. They are delicious, but they make me very thirsty. I like to drink fresh orange juice with them. Orange juice is the best drink in Israel. We grow lots of oranges here.

90

Sometimes soldiers sit at the tables, eating. Some are men and some are women. They all have guns. They have to carry guns because some of the countries near Israel are not friendly and do not want to live peacefully with us.

When I grow up, I will be in the army. My sisters will go into the army, too. Everyone goes to the army for three years, right after high school. We all have to learn to protect our country in case of war. But we always pray for peace.

We have had four terrible wars since Israel became a state. Some of my family's friends and some of our relatives were killed in these wars. I hope there will never be another war.

This picture of Tel Aviv was taken from Jaffa.
You can see how close — and how different — they are.

El Al is Israel's national airline.

Just outside of Tel Aviv is Ben Gurion Airport. When Uncle Avram travels by plane from America to Israel, he lands at Ben Gurion Airport. He says the El Al planes that belong to Israel are very good. He boards the plane in the evening and arrives in Tel Aviv the next day. It is always exciting when Uncle Avram comes. He brings a suitcase full of surprises for me — things to play with and things to eat. The last time, he brought me some American bubble gum and a big map of the United States.

I like maps; they are interesting and important. My father makes maps for the Israel Government. That is his job. Since Israel

92

became a state in 1948, our borders have changed three times. My father has to make perfect maps that show all the changes. Then he has to write about the land and explain where the mountains and valleys and plains are, and what kind of rocks and soil they are made of. Some of his maps show where there is water, where there are forests, and what kinds of plants grow in different parts of the land.

I learn about this in school during geography class, but it's more fun to learn it from my father. Father taught me that Israel is a part of the continent called Asia, and even though it is a tiny country, it touches four seas. They are the Red Sea, the Dead

Tel Aviv has grown, and is a very crowded city.

Potash from the Dead Sea is shipped all over the world. It is used for fertilizer.

These "statues" were formed by natu from the salt in the Dead Sea.

Sea, the Sea of Galilee (which we call **Kinneret**, because that means "harp" and that is how it is shaped), and the Mediterranean Sea. The Dead Sea is the lowest place in the whole world, almost a mile below sea level. The water tastes terrible, because it is full of salt and other minerals. Some of the minerals in the Dead Sea are important, and are shipped all over the world. Nothing can live in the Dead Sea — that's how it got its name — but flowers and vegetables grow right alongside it!

Date palms grow near the Dead Sea, but beautiful orchards with orange, lemon and grapefruit trees grow near my home in Tel Aviv!

94

My friends at school think I am very smart when I share what my father has taught me. My father is a very good teacher. He teaches me lots of things other than geography. He tells me good stories about King David and King Solomon. I sit very still, listening; I try not to move. And when he finishes his stories, I dream of what it would have been like if I had lived long ago, in the time of King David or King Solomon . . . .

It's fun to go shopping in Tel Aviv.

95

A WORD SQUARE IN DIZENGOFF CIRCLE

Dizengoff Circle is so crowded that the letters in this square got squeezed together. Can you find 15 words and names that you have read in the chapter about Tel Aviv?

Read across, up and down, and diagonally. Circle each word that you find.

```
S D T A R M Y C S L F
O B E N G U R I O N E
L M L A R N E T R J L
D S A T D E D Y A A A
I Q V P R S S U N F F
E P I T A L E F G F E
R N V R N B A A E A L
C P D I Z E N G O F F
D A I R P O R T O L T
```

Did you find all these words?

Tel Aviv   city   Jaffa   Dizengoff   felafel   pita   orange
soldier   Ben Gurion   map   Red Sea   tree   Dead Sea   army
airport

CAN YOU TELL ABOUT TEL AVIV?

If you can complete these sentences correctly, you will know a great deal about Tel Aviv.

1 Tel Aviv is on the _____ Sea.

2 It is a very big and crowded city with many _____ and museums.

3 The suburb of _____ was an ancient port.

4 In sunny weather people like to eat at _____ cafes.

5 _____ Circle was named after Tel Aviv's first mayor.

6 Everyone in Israel goes into the _____ after finishing high school.

7 Israel has had four _____ ; we hope there will not be another one.

8 _____ Airport is near Tel Aviv.

9 Israel grows many juicy _____.

10 Tehina, humus and pita are _____ foods that everyone likes.

You can check your answers on p. 127.

TEL AVIV, MY HOME

MAP STUDY 1

Here's a map that Gershon's father made. It shows where the hills are in Israel and where there is water.

Here are some names that belong on the map. Write the names in the correct place on the map and then color the page.

Negev
Galilee
Mount Carmel
Dead Sea
Red Sea
Sea of Galilee
Mediterranean Sea

98

I LIVE IN ISRAEL

MAP STUDY 2

Gershon's father also made this map of Israel. He left dots to show the location of some of Israel's main cities. Next to each dot is a blank line. Can you complete the map by writing in the name of each city?

If you can complete the sentences below, they will help you.

1 _____ is a seaport in the north of Israel.

2 _____ and _____ are a city and a suburb on the Mediterranean.

3 _____, the capital, is in the center of Israel.

4 _____ is high in the mountains, near the Sea of Galilee.

5 _____ is the most important city in the Negev.

6 _____ is a resort city on the Red Sea.

99

JERUSALEM, 964 B.C.E.

10

JERUSALEM, MY HOME

IN THE YEAR 964 B.C.E.

MY NAME is Nehemiah and I live in Jerusalem. Solomon is my king, and I think he is a very good king. My father works for the king in the copper mines of Timnah, in the Negeb Desert. Mother and I do not see him a lot, for it takes him weeks to get home from the mines. We would go to live near him, but there is no place for us to stay at the mines. Here in Jerusalem we have a nice home.

Our home has one room with walls made of stone, Built into the floor, we have a stone oven where we cook our food. In the corner there is a clay water jar which my mother carries to the well every day to fill.

My mother told me that King Solomon, who has been our king for three years, plans to build a great Temple to the Lord. He will begin next year. He is thinking about building it on the highest place in the city, a mountain called Moriah. Everywhere we go, people are talking about the new Temple. Maybe my

100

father will come back from the mines and help to build the new Temple.

Every day soldiers bring strong horses into Jerusalem. They will have to work very hard to pull the huge stones into place for the Temple walls. It is good that the horses are so strong.

Mother said that kings from many lands were sending precious gifts for the new Temple. King Hiram of Tyre shipped huge cedar trees from Lebanon to be cut into lumber for the Temple. Other kings are sending gold and silver. It will be melted down to make bowls and candelabra and decorations for the Ark of the Law.

King Solomon's copper mines were near here.

101

My mother will help to decorate the Temple. She is a very good seamstress and she will help to sew the costly linen from Egypt into curtains for the Temple. The curtains will hang on rods made of olive wood.

I will work too. I will have to take care of my two younger sisters, Shula and Deborah, while my mother is sewing curtains. I will not mind too much because it will give me a chance to practice my reading.

No one in my family knows how to read. It is not supposed to be important for us to read, so we were never taught. But I want to learn very much, and wish that I could go to a school to study, so that I could become a scribe. A scribe is a person who reads and writes for other people.

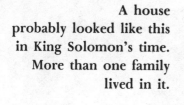

A house probably looked like this in King Solomon's time. More than one family lived in it.

I LIVE IN ISRAEL

יְרוּשָׁלַ‍ִם

This is how we write
"Jerusalem"
in modern Hebrew.

ylwyaz

This is how "Jerusalem"
was written in the
time of King Solomon.

This is how a scribe writes a Torah scroll today.

Someday I would like to read the Laws of the Torah to my father, and read about the Ten Tribes of Israel to my sisters. I might even write about a boy my own age, but he would be a boy of the future. He would live 3,000 years from now, and he would look just like me and talk just like me. He would have fine clothes and a large clean home to live in. He would have different foods to eat every day and there would always be enough food in his house so that he would never be hungry. His mother would never be tired, and his father would work close to home and would play with him each day.

3,000 years from now, things would be very different . . . .

103

JERUSALEM, 964 B.C.E.

A HISTORICAL CROSSWORD PUZZLE

Across:

1 _____ worshipped in King Solomon's Temple

2 This kind of tree grew in Lebanon

5 This chapter took us back in _____

6 Animals that can pull heavy loads

8 What Nehemiah wanted to be

9 Another word for hard work

10 Nehemiah's father worked in a copper _____ in Timnah

11 Hill on which Solomon built the Temple

12 Water from the eye

Down:

1 Solomon built the Temple here

3 Forever and _____

4 A boy who lived in Jerusalem in the time of King Solomon

5 King Hiram of _____ sent cedars for the Temple

7 Other kings sent gold and _____ as gifts

9 Bedouin live in a _____

104

You can check your answers on page 127.

JERUSALEM, 964 B.C.E.

HOME FOR THE HOLIDAY

Nehemiah's father is coming home for the festival of Shavuot. But first he has to find his way out of the copper mine.

There are many tunnels, but only one leads to the outside. Can you help Nehemiah's father find the right one?

106

WHAT'S WRONG IN THIS PICTURE?

Here's a picture of what Nehemiah's home must have been like so many years ago. But somehow the artist has made a few mistakes and some things which are modern slipped into the picture.

Can you circle the modern things that don't belong in this ancient household?

107

JERUSALEM, 964 B.C.E.

11

JERUSALEM, MY HOME

WHAT IT MIGHT BE LIKE IN THE YEAR 2000

MY NAME is Ariela. I live in Jerusalem with my father and mother and brother in a four-room apartment. My mother is a reporter on the city's newspaper, THE JERUSALEM POST. My father works at the Shalom Museum. I can see the museum's gardens from our apartment. My father is in charge of the museum and trains all the guides. He teaches them how to explain about the museum, and about **shalom**, which means "peace."

Just a few years ago, peace came to Israel and the whole Middle East. I can't remember that, because I wasn't born then. But my father told me to go through the museum with the guides, and to listen and learn. The first thing I learned is that Israel had many wars. In each war, many brave young people died, and the Israelis were very sad. The Arab countries lost many good people, too, and they were very sad.

In the Shalom Museum are weapons that were used for fighting wars long ago: swords, spears, bows, arrows. And weapons used not too long ago: machine guns, tanks, airplanes, bombs. Really,

108

the Shalom Museum could have been called a War Museum, because it shows all the terrible things that war has done. It is sad to know that people had to go to war, even when they saw how much unhappiness war caused.

I am glad there are no more wars now. Would you like to know how peace came about? Here is the story I heard.

★

Once the leaders of the countries came together for a meeting. They each complained that their lands were being ruined because there were not enough strong men and women to care for them. So many men and women had died, that there were not enough babies being born.

Can you read the Hebrew on this sign?

109

This woodcut is by Mordecai Cohen who lives in Beersheva. He calls it "Two Friends".

9

First the leaders tried to agree on a peace settlement that would be fair to everyone. But they couldn't agree. Then they had an idea. From now on, they declared, only old men and old women would be allowed to fight in wars. Young men and women would stay home and raise babies and work and take care of the land.

For a while there were no wars. Then little fights became big fights, and there was a new war between the Arabs and the Israelis. Now only the old people went out to fight. Some bad things and some good things happened. One bad thing was that the old people could not move very fast, and soldiers must move fast in a war. One good thing was that the old people could only fight about three hours a day before they would get tired. Still, it was a real war, and the leaders knew that this was not a wise answer to their problem.

After the War of the Old, the leaders met again. They agreed that young men and women should not fight and they agreed that old men and women should not fight. So there was only one thing left to do. Little children would be sent out to fight. When the children heard about this, they were very sad. They felt it was unfair that they had not been given a vote in this important decision. But no one paid any attention to them.

Soon people began to treat each other badly again, and another war began. This time all the parents and grandparents kissed the children and sent them off to fight. They gave each child a

111

change of clothes, a sack of food, a large rifle, and a bag of bullets.

It was just too much to carry. So the first thing the children did was to drop those heavy bullets. Now it was easier to walk. But as they were walking, someone said, "Why are we carrying these rifles when we have no bullets to put in them?"

"That's right," said another child, and everyone threw away the guns.

The first night the children were very tired and they slept very well. The next morning they put on fresh clothing and picked up their sacks of food and continued to march off to war. At lunchtime they saw the enemy children.

112

But when they looked at the enemy, they saw that the enemy children must have had the same problems. No one had a gun and no one had any bullets. All they had was a lot of food. Someone called out, "Do you want to have lunch with us?" And soon all the children, Arabs and Israelis, were sitting down and sharing their food.

That night they shared their blankets, too, and everyone slept quietly. But by morning some of the smallest children began to cry. They wanted to go home. And at last, though it was fun to play together, everyone agreed that it was time to go home.

This woodcut was made by Nabil Abdul Madjid who lives in Abu Ghosh. It shows his visit to Kibbutz Kiryat Anavim.

Just before they left, the Arab children made a promise, and the Israeli children made a promise, that they would never fight against each other again, as long as they lived.

When they came marching home, they found their parents crying. Everyone was afraid that his or her child might be hurt. But then, when they saw that no one was hurt at all, they laughed and laughed. And everyone was happy because there would never be a war again.

Sometimes people would become angry, but then the children would take them into the fields for a picnic and would sit and talk to them. They would eat some cake together and drink some fresh water from the stream. When they came back home, they had forgotten war completely.

And that is why the older people built the Shalom Museum to show how terrible and foolish war really is.

*

That is the story just the way I heard it. But, as I say, it all happened before I was born. I think I am very lucky because my father is in charge of this important museum. Now while I am small, I talk to older people who are angry, and share a piece of cake with them. When I grow up, I will work in the Shalom Museum like my father, and my children will remind us that we should never fight wars again.

114

THE JERUSALEM POST

THURSDAY, VOL. XLIX, No. 14631 IL13.00 (inc. Vat)

Soviet Jews
*
Page 3

Righteous Gentiles to be honoured

The Righteous Gentiles medallion, the highest honour bestowed by the State of Israel upon a non-Jew, will be awarded posthumously to Janina and Franciszek Cygan, of Poland, during a tree planting ceremony tomorrow at Jerusalem's Yad Vashem Holocaust memorial

The Cygan family
Sara

Cabinet marathon continues; approval of peace draft seen

Israel reports breakthrough

Com majority expected in cabinet

By ASHER WALLFISH and MARK SEGAL
Jerusalem Post Reporters

A comfortable — rity is comment

welcome in Jerusalem

between the offspring of Ishmael and Isaac at the home of the patriarch, Abraham, where the new covenant of peace would be fortified.
sheba, the desert capital, its day in the sun. Despite ive growth and centre of com- an industrial wastes.

Been given never

Haifa celebrated zest and initiative with children in fancy dress while traffic slowed to a crawl.

peace mission

At 2 p.m. a municipality football squad, captained by Mayor Arye Gurel, played a scrimmage against a Technion team on the lawn of Gan Hazikaron. The friendly game was 31-degree heat.
the Egyptian leader.

war of Attrition. It is the three that does facilities.

Dalia
To loud applause
assembly of over 1,000,
that when all is said and
stand alone. We have only one ally
Ho He said the American Jewish community was the most influential in the world.
the Jewish community full of
are imports, and display
find in the Old City
more expensive. F
minute ride through
woods will tak
place of a
Arabic n

on the slope
held his contest
Baal. First
the prophet
persua to assemble
the idola how he instructed them, build altars and offer sacrifices, challenging them to

was what Elijah must have to produce such an effect. to say his efforts were

The prime minister said cabinet confirmation he would last night that after ment to the Knesset next week for approval. He

Muhraka is the solitary the beginning Ca guard there, monks and a hou Sudah. Their water has from neighbouring Dalia, supply of electricity com erator; and they there

everything.
mountains, the w
us."

Ask Sudah to open the monastery's terrace for you. The view is too for words. Your eyes s far as Lebanon to the he east the whole of el and the mountains of and right across the Jor. One-third of Israel is ur feet. Close by, there well-kept picnic sites, sur- several of Salah Sudah's tures.
a kilometre further up the aches Haifa University. years old — the younges ntry — it wa
Bra

peace treaty seen a

are open
from 10:00 a.m. to noon
4:00 p.m. to 6:00 p.m. with no entrance fee. A short walk uphill will take you to the Peace Garden and Lookout containing 18 sculptures dona he city by Ursula Malbin. you come to Hadar with its museums, its entertainment spots.
first non-Arab neighbourhood to be built in Haifa, the old German Colony, is still there with man original stone houses generally the distr neglected. Th right a goo

JERUSALEM POST POLL
Most Israelis tru

the moun ral kilometres of line, with a choice of unicipal beaches, some also viding playgrounds for children. mall marina, by the Kishon here yacht owners and go sailing up to kra cliffs. cipal
put Haifa to their w

local
head of the
more than 3,000 hotel room
the demand. We are doing all
promotion we can and visitors are
coming to the city. But where are we
going to lodge them?"

VOICE OF PEACE
"This is the second gre
my life," said
"The fi

Nationwide festivities star

לקראת שלום במזרח התיכון

نحو السلام في الشرق الأوسط

TOWARDS PEACE IN THE MIDDLE EAST

concerts and late-night dancing outdoors. The Beersheba Symphony Orchestra and Repertory Theatre gave special performances, while galleries and shops in the "old city," under renovation as a Jaffa-like cultural centre, mounted special "peace exhibitions."

It was a time of pomp and ceremony, more than a little astray from the shirt-sleeve image of this frontier town. There were the

ed large clouds of brown dust as they ferried VIPs in and out of the Hundreds of newsmen them in Beersheba for th scurried around the p barking out stories telephone hook-ups to places. Thousands of soldiers and policemen cordoned off large sections of the city and virtually turned this desert city into a garrison town.

It was a time of remembrance.

תזמורת סימפונית ירושלים
JERUSALEM SYMPHONY ORCHESTRA

GARY BERTINI CHIEF CONDUCTOR & MUSICAL DIRECTOR

university is so
that even far below the
fa

useful purpose.
width was strung a huge, handpainted banner that read, "Nation shall not lift up sword against nation, neither shall they learn war any more."

THE PEACE PICNIC

Here's the place where the Peace Picnic happened, according to Ariela's story. But no one has arrived yet. Draw many children — Arab and Israeli — having a good time.

GOING HOME

Help the children get home from the Peace Picnic by taking them through the maze. There are two children — and they start out together, but then each one takes a different path to get home.

Do you know which house belongs to which child?

JERUSALEM, IN 2000

A PEACE STAMP

The Israel post office of the future wants to issue a new stamp to celebrate the coming of peace to the Middle East. Can you help to design a Peace Stamp?

Here is space for you to write a poem or a short story about your ideas of peace.

_____

_____

_____

_____

ISRAEL, OUR HOME

IF YOU ARE JEWISH, you have more than one home. You may live in the United States, in Canada, in England, or in South Africa, but Israel has a special place in your heart. All of the places you have read about — the kibbutz, the cities, Israel long ago, and the peaceful Israel we pray for — all these belong to you, too. They belong to you because you are a Jew.

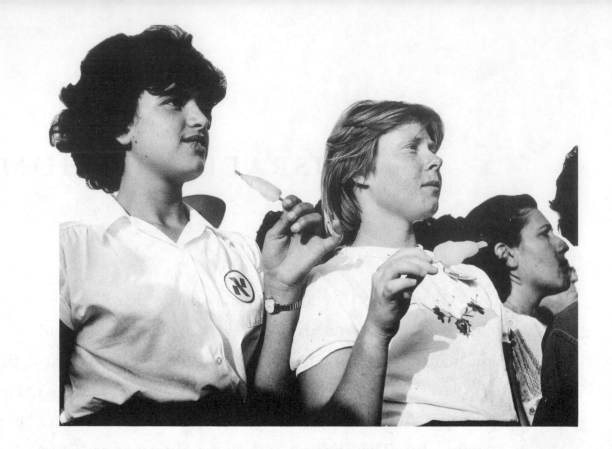

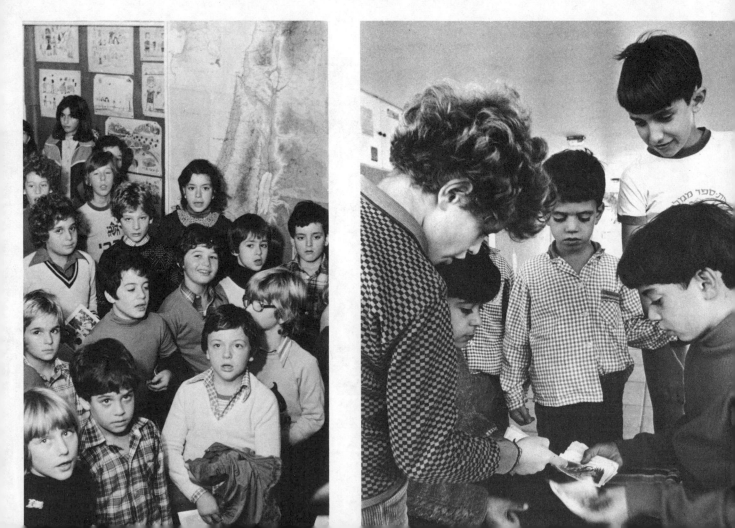

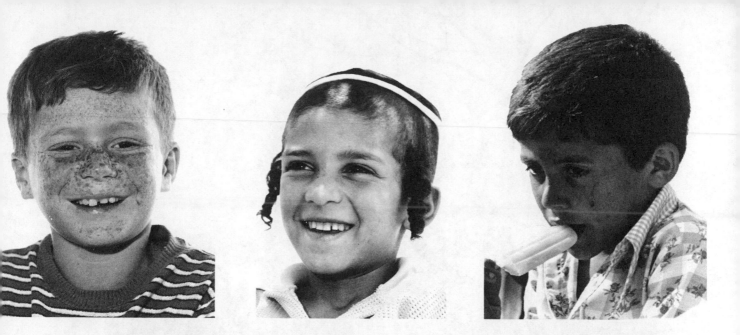

You may never live in Israel, but Israel should always live in you. You have learned about the Land of Israel (**Eretz Yisrael**) and about the State of Israel (**Medinat Yisrael**). There is also another Israel — the People of Israel (**Am Yisrael**). Wherever you may live in the world, you will always be a part of the people of Israel, because you are a Jew. Wherever you live, you and we in Israel are one big family.

We hope you will learn a great deal about Israel, and about being a Jew. The more you know, the more you will be able to help Israel remain a strong country, where all the children will grow up in a peaceful world. Then you and we, together, will help make the world a better place in which to live.

So, from Yosi, Avi, Moshe, Tova, Saul, Aliza, Ettie, Gershon, Nehemiah and Ariela — from all of us in Israel to all of you — good luck and שָׁלוֹם !

עַם יִשְׂרָאֵל · אֶרֶץ יִשְׂרָאֵל · מְדִינַת יִשְׂרָאֵל

ISRAEL — OUR HOME

Here is a map of Israel showing all the places you have been reading about. Now that you know something about these places, where would you like to live in Israel?

Draw a circle around the place you have chosen, and write your reasons for choosing it.

_____

_____

_____

_____

_____

_____

_____

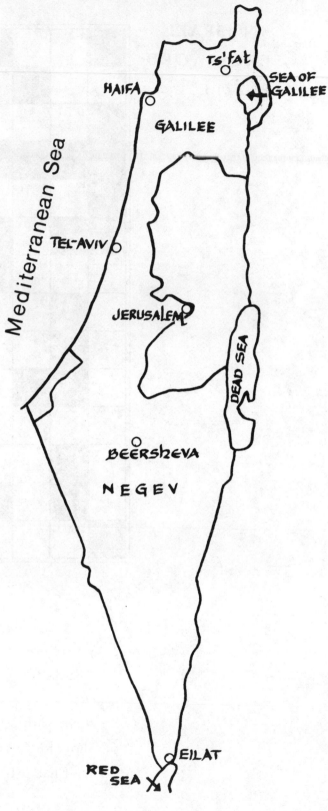

AN ISRAEL CROSSWORD PUZZLE

Down

1. _____ Shearim

2. Where everyone shares the work

3. A suburb on the Mediterranean Sea, that used to be the main city

4. A city with a C-shaped harbor

6. Short for father

7. Fruit hangs from the branch by its _____

9   A city in the Negev

11   A port on the Red Sea

12   The northern part of Israel is called _____

15   A Hebrew word meaning "look-out"

16   Name for someone born in Israel; also, the fruit of the cactus

18   _____ **Sea**

21   Old name for the city of Akko

24   _____ Aviv

Across

1   Israel, _____ Home

3   A_____ has a special **feeling** about Israel

5   I like him, and he likes _____

6   Flat Arab bread

7   Mediterranean _____

8   Tehina and humus are _____ foods.

9   A kind of meat

10   Capital of the Jewish State

12   Another word for girl

13   The Jewish State

14   Near, or next to

17   City in Upper Galilee

19   Name for the desert in the south of Israel

20   Every tree has a different shape of _____

22   Grows in the waters of the Red Sea

23   Same as 14 across

25   What Jews and Arabs need; also what **shalom** means

26   Newcomers to the Jewish State

You can check your answers on p. 127.

125

ISRAEL, OUR HOME

THE LAST WORD

The people of Israel have a final message for you. To find out what it is, fill in the blanks, and then read the word spelled out by the letters inside the circles.

1 The Jewish State   _ Ⓞ _ _ _

2 An important city in the Negev   _ _ _ _ _ Ⓞ _ _

3 A city next to Jaffa   _ _ Ⓞ _ _ _

4 The Hebrew word for "newcomers"   _ Ⓞ _ _

5 David's son   _ _ _ Ⓞ _ _ _

6 Israel, My   _ _ Ⓞ _

שָׁלוֹם !

You can check your answer on page 127.

I LIVE IN ISRAEL

ANSWER PAGE

p. 22   *Across:* 3 women   4 mother   5 kibbutz   8 farm   10 care   11 Hagalil
         Down: 1 northern   2 home   3 work   6 Israel   7 zoo   9 rest

p. 35   1 capital   3 laws   5 protection   7 pray   9 mosque
         2 middle   4 Arabs   6 King   8 doing evil   10 Wall

p. 48   *Across:* 1 wall   6 trees   10 Yad   13 meal   19 Isaac
              3 Old City   8 home   11 Moslem   16 New   20 forest

         Down: 2 Abraham   5 Temple   9 Holy   12 Museum   15 hair   18 near
               4 Law   8 Solomon   11 Ma   14 alef   17 was   19 it

p. 58   1 Abraham's   4 sheep and goats   7 the first Hebrew   10 Isaac
         2 4,000 years old   5 in the fields   8 his father's idols
         3 stones   6 in Beersheva   9 the one God

p. 68   1 Eilat   3 Morocco   5 ship   7 ships   9 hot
         2 swimming   4 fish   6 reefs   8 caught   10 vacation

p. 88   1 Galilee   3 look out   5 bonfires   7 prayers   9 artists
         2 mountain   4 health   6 Lion   8 synagogues   10 Sabra
                                                        11 Ladino

p. 97   1 Mediterranean   3 Jaffa   5 Dizengoff   7 wars   9 oranges
         2 theatres   4 outdoor   6 army   8 Ben Gurion   10 Arab

p. 104   *Across:* 1 Jews   5 time   8 scribe   10 Mine   12 tear
           2 cedar   6 horses   9 toil   11 Moriah
         Down: 1 Jerusalem   3 ever   4 Nehemiah   5 Tyre   7 silver   9 tent

p. 124   *Across:* 1 my   7 sea   12 gal   19 Negev   26 olim
           3 Jew   8 Arab   13 Israel   20 leaf
           5 me   9 beef   14 at   22 coral
           6 pita   10 Jerusalem   17 Tsfat   25 peace

         Down: 1 Mea   4 Haifa   9 Beersheva   15 tsafo   21 Acre
            2 kibbutz   6 pa   11 Eilat   16 sabra   24 Tel
            3 Jaffa   7 stem   12 Galilee   18 Red

p. 126   1 Israel   3 Tel Aviv   5 Solomon   *Message:*
          2 Beersheva   4 olim   6 home   SHALOM!

127